MATHS MAGIC

Shape and Pattern

Written by Wendy Clemson
and David Clemson

LONDON ■ PRINCETON
www.two-canpublishing.com

Published by Two-Can Publishing
43-45 Dorset Street, London W1U 7NA

www.two-canpublishing.com

© Two-Can Publishing 2001

For information on Two-Can books and multimedia,
call (0)20 7224 2440, fax (0)20 7224 7005
or visit our website at http://www.two-canpublishing.com

Created by
act-two
346 Old Street
London EC1V 9RB

Authors: Wendy Clemson and David Clemson

Editor: Penny Smith
Designer: Helen Holmes
Illustrators: Andy Peters and Mike Stones
Photographer: Daniel Pangbourne
Pre-press production: Adam Wilde

'Two-Can' is a trademark of Two-Can Publishing.
Two-Can Publishing is a division of Zenith Entertainment plc,
43-45 Dorset Street, London W1U 7NA

Hardback ISBN 1-85434-876-0
Paperback ISBN 1-85434-877-9

Dewey Decimal Classification 516

Hardback 10 9 8 7 6 5 4 3 2 1
Paperback 10 9 8 7 6 5 4 3 2 1

A catalogue record for this book is available
from the British Library.

Colour reproduction by the Graphic Facilities Group
Printed in Hong Kong

Contents

Shape spotting

Our world is full of all kinds o
shapes. Look at this fairgrour
There are things made from
shapes and shapes with straig
and pointed corners. When sl
repeated, they make fantastic

4

Find these shapes in the picture.

Can you find different coloured shapes that fit together to make patterns?

5

The four-sided family

Do all the shapes in the big picture have four sides? Shapes with four sides and four corners are called quadrilaterals. A square has sides that are all the same length and corners that match.
Try to describe the sides and corners of an oblong.

Cut out a collection of four-sided shapes

YOU WILL NEED
paper, scissors, ruler

1 Use straight cuts to make your shapes. Try to make them different from each other, but remember they must all have four sides.

Top tip
When you cut a square from corner to corner, each piece is exactly half.

oblong

square

2 Do any of your shapes have sides that are the same length? Measure them with a ruler to find out. Do any of your shapes look similar to the shapes in the big picture?

6

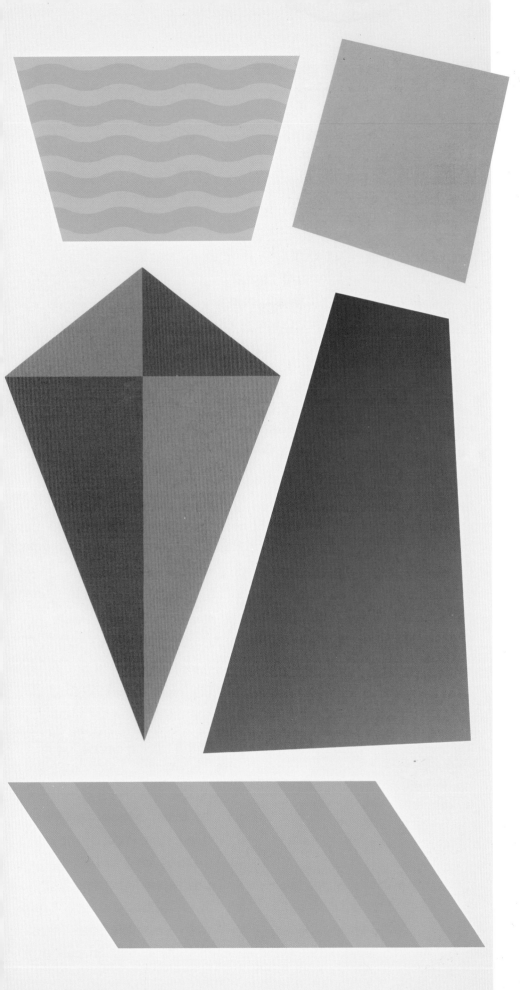

BRAIN teaser

Challenge a friend to turn six squares into three by removing three matches.

There are six squares in this shape, five small ones and one big one with four small squares inside.

Which three matches will you take away to make three squares?

Hey presto! Now the shape has three squares.

7

Triangles

Do you know why a triangle is called a tri-angle? It's because it has three straight sides and three corners, or angles. There are different kinds of triangles. You can have fun making triangles into pictures and new shapes with straight sides.

Make a picture from triangles

YOU WILL NEED
scissors, coloured paper or card, glue

1 Cut out different types of triangles in all kinds of sizes and colours.

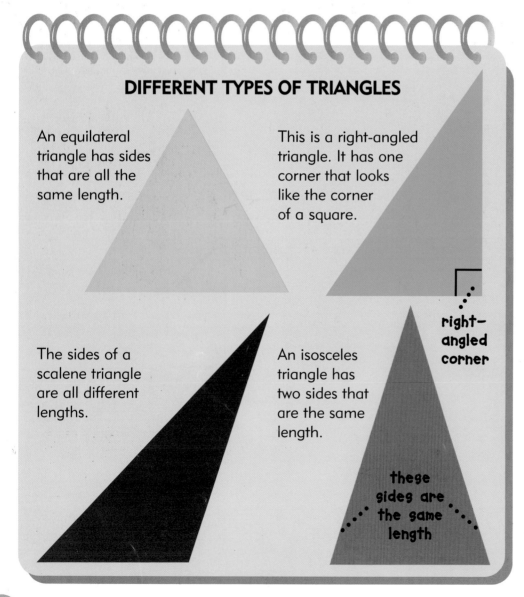

DIFFERENT TYPES OF TRIANGLES

An equilateral triangle has sides that are all the same length.

This is a right-angled triangle. It has one corner that looks like the corner of a square.

right-angled corner

The sides of a scalene triangle are all different lengths.

An isosceles triangle has two sides that are the same length.

these sides are the same length

2 On a piece of paper or card, place the triangles next to each other to make a picture full of new shapes and colourful patterns. Experiment, then when you are happy with your picture, glue the triangles in place.

PROVE IT!

There's something magical about a right-angled triangle. The two small corners fit exactly into the biggest corner! See for yourself.

mark the smaller corners

Cut out a right-angled triangle from the corner of a piece of paper.

Next simply cut off the marked corners.

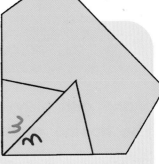

Then put them in the biggest corner. They fit perfectly!

Match that shape

You'll be amazed at how many different shapes there are. Play this game to practise naming and matching shapes. Here's a winning tip. Look at the shape box below and try to remember the number of sides and matching sides of each shape.

SHAPE BOX

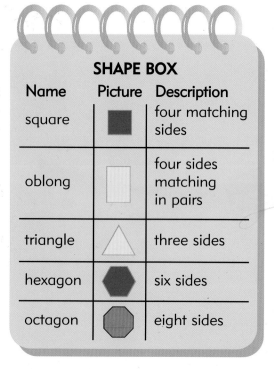

Name	Picture	Description
square		four matching sides
oblong		four sides matching in pairs
triangle		three sides
hexagon		six sides
octagon		eight sides

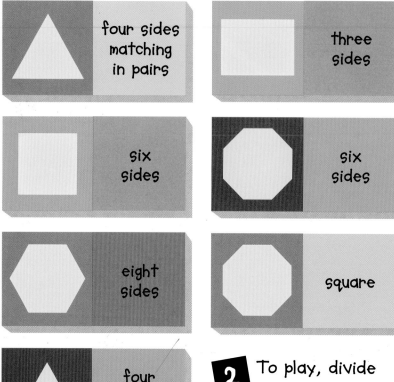

four sides matching in pairs

three sides

six sides

six sides

eight sides

square

four matching sides

four sides matching in pairs

2 To play, divide the dominoes equally between two players. The first player to go puts down a domino.

four matching sides

three sides

Make and play the domino game

YOU WILL NEED
card, scissors, felt pens

1 Make a set of 14 dominoes like the ones shown here.

triangle

oblong

octagon

hexagon

3 The next player matches a domino to the one on the floor. The match is by name, picture or description. Take turns. The player left with the least dominoes is the winner.

Now try this
BRAIN teaser

Here's a chance to show star quality! Challenge a friend to make one five-sided shape, called a pentagon, inside another.

First draw a pentagon, then draw a line from one corner to another.

Now join all the other corners. Here's your star, but what else can you see? There's a new pentagon in the centre!

four sides matching in pairs

four matching sides

octagon

three sides

six sides

square

eight sides

six sides

Turning around

As time passes, the hands on a clock turn in one direction. This is called clockwise. If time could go backwards, the hands would turn the other way. This direction is anti-clockwise. A spiral is also a kind of turn. It starts in the middle and turns further and further away from where it started.

clockwise

anti-clockwise

Wow!

Water drains out of your bath in an anti-clockwise direction. But if you were in Australia it would drain clockwise!

Decorate cakes with spiral patterns

1 Pipe writing icing in spirals on little cakes. Start in the middle. On one cake, make the spiral clockwise. On another cake, make it anti-clockwise.

YOU WILL NEED
ready-to-use writing icing, cakes, sweets

clockwise spiral

anti-clockwise spiral

The edge of a circle is the same distance from the centre all the way around. To check draw a circle. Fold it in half and half again, then unfold it. The centre is where the fold lines cross. Now measure.

2 Decorate a big cake with colourful spirals and sweets. Practise on paper first. What pictures are you going to make?

13

Right angles

When you spin right round on your feet, you make a complete turn and end up where you started. But when you move in a quarter turn, you change direction. A right angle is a quarter turn. There are four right angles in a square, one at each corner.

Top tip

Make a right-angle tester to check the angles in your maze. Fold a piece of paper – or even a leaf – in half. Then fold it again so the first fold lines up.

Make a right-angled maze

1 Cut out at least 24 squares of paper. The squares should all have 6 cm sides.

YOU WILL NEED
scissors, paper, coloured tape

2 Make guide lines by folding each square in half, then half again. Unfold the squares. Use coloured tape to copy the patterns shown at the top of the next page. Use your guide lines to position the tape accurately.

PROVE IT!

To make a complete turn you have to turn through four right angles, or quarter turns. In the picture, how many times has the man changed direction? What shape is he making?

start here

14

Copy the patterns on these squares

3 Now lay out your squares so the coloured tape makes roads in the maze. Trace a finger around the maze. How many right-angled turns can you make?

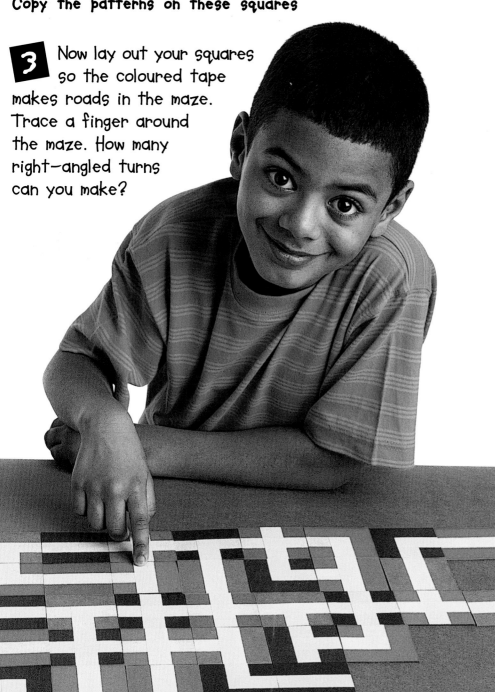

Now try this

BRAIN teaser

Challenge a friend to see how many right-angled triangles she can make from one oblong.

One way is to draw a line like this. Now there are two right-angled triangles.

A better way is to draw three lines. This makes four right-angled triangles.

fold and cut

What happens when you fold a piece of paper in half then cut a shape on the fold? Experiment with fold and cut shapes to find out. Before you open them out, think how they will look. Are they the same or different to how you imagined?

2 These shapes have been cut out. Which pieces of cut paper belong together?

Cut out folded shapes

YOU WILL NEED
paper, scissors

1 Fold a sheet of paper and make a single cut across the two layers. Open the paper. What shape do you have? Now try making two, three and four cuts. What shapes have you cut out?

Now try this

BRAIN teaser

Challenge a friend to make a paper man into eight men!

fold .... outer edges

....outer edges

folds

First, fold a thin piece of square paper in half, then fold it in half again to make a smaller square.

Next, fold the paper from corner to corner. Make sure that the outer edges are all together.

Now draw a picture of just one man. His arms and legs must reach right to the folds in the paper.

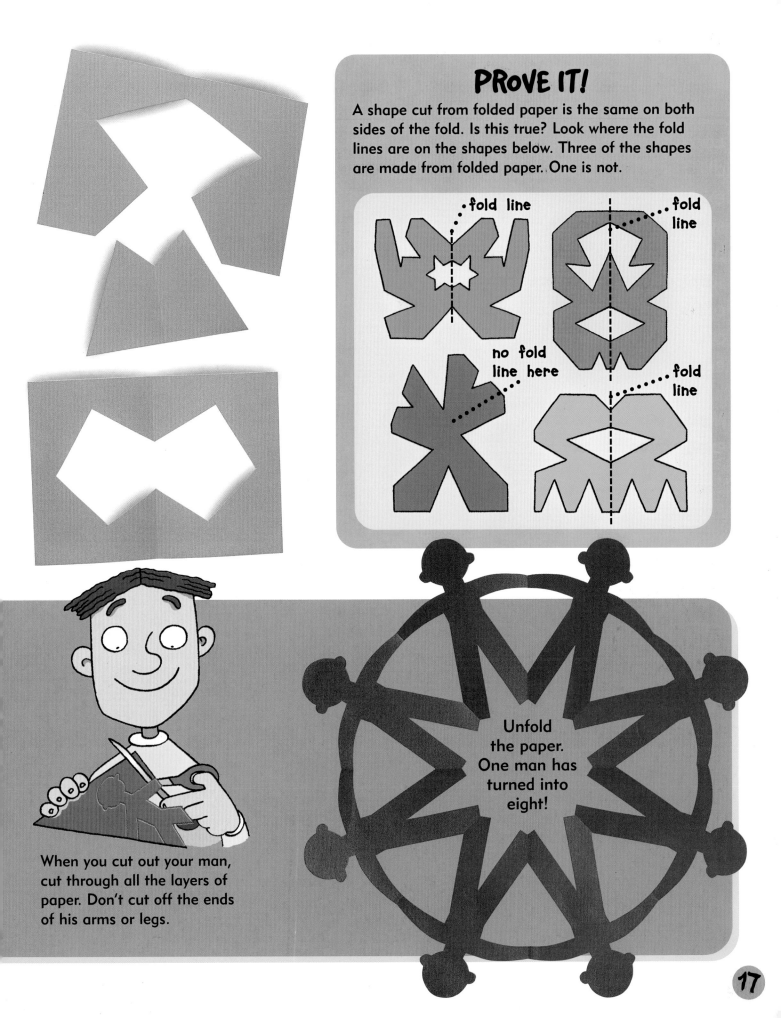

PROVE IT!

A shape cut from folded paper is the same on both sides of the fold. Is this true? Look where the fold lines are on the shapes below. Three of the shapes are made from folded paper. One is not.

fold line

fold line

no fold line here

fold line

Unfold the paper. One man has turned into eight!

When you cut out your man, cut through all the layers of paper. Don't cut off the ends of his arms or legs.

17

Half and half

Look at the big shark. A fold line divides it into two halves that match exactly. This is called the line of symmetry. Check that both halves of the shark are the same. Count the number of teeth, eyes and fins in each half.

line of symmetry

Make a symmetrical card

YOU WILL NEED
card, pencil, scissors, glue

1 Fold a piece of card in half. Draw half a picture right up to the fold line.

2 Cut out your card and make sure it will stand up. Then write your message on the back.

BRAIN teaser

fold line

Challenge a friend to double the number of biscuits on a plate. Here's how to make it work.

First draw a picture of a plate and cut it out. Fold the plate in half, then unfold it.

Draw and colour in a handful of biscuits on one side of the fold.

Hold a mirror along the fold. Now you can see twice the number of biscuits you had before!

3 Make up your own symmetrical picture cards. Decorate them with coloured shapes and patterns.

PROVE IT!

A shape can have more than one line of symmetry. The top pictures have several, while the middle pictures have one each. Prove this by holding a mirror along the lines to see if the reflections match. The bottom pictures have no lines of symmetry.

lines of symmetry

no lines of symmetry here

Pin pictures

Everything you see has a shape. Many shapes have straight sides. Make your own shapes and patterns with wool and a pinboard. How many different shapes can you make?

Make and use a pinboard

YOU WILL NEED
ruler, pencil, polystyrene, pins, wool

1 Draw a grid of squares on thick polystyrene with about six squares along each side. The squares should measure about 3 cm x 3 cm.

2 The next part is tricky, so ask an adult to help. Push pins through the corners of the squares. Make sure the pins are securely in place.

3 Knot the wool around one pin and wind it around others to make a shape. Tie a knot. Make as many shapes as you can.

4 Now make patterns of squares that touch along at least one side. Try making these using two, three, four and five squares.

PROVE IT!

These patterns are made up of four squares that touch along at least one side. You can make five different patterns this way. Four are shown here. The fifth is on the pinboard above. Can you find it?

BRAIN teaser

Wind wool around any square on your pinboard. The number of pins inside the square is a square number. Challenge a friend to work out some square numbers.

First get your friend to wind wool around four pins to make a small square. This shows that four is a square number.

What is the next square number? Count the pins and you will see that it is nine.

What about the next? This square number is 16. Use your pinboard to work out more square numbers.

21

Three dimensions

A flat shape, such as a square, has length and width. These are called the two dimensions. A cube, or square box, has three dimensions. It has length, width and depth. Make a cube from an arrangement of flat squares, called a net.

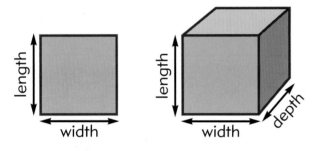

Make and decorate a cube picture box

YOU WILL NEED
card, ruler, pencil, scissors, tape, photographs, glue

1 On card draw a square with sides of about 8 cm. Cut it out. Copy the pattern shown below by drawing around your cut-out square. Make sure the squares in the pattern touch.

PROVE IT!

On this page, there are five different ways to arrange your squares to make a net for a cube. Can you see them? To make sure that each net works, copy it, cut it out and make it into a little box.

2 Now cut around the outside of the shape.

Top tip

A dice is a cube. It has six faces, or flat surfaces. This is easy to remember because the highest number is six.

3 Fold the shape along the lines of the squares to make a cube. Tape the cube together.

4 Cut your favourite photographs to size, then stick them to the faces of the cube.

Cylinders and Cones

Shapes with curved surfaces roll. The surface of a round ball, or sphere, is completely curved. Cones and cylinders also have curved surfaces, but they have flat faces, too, which means they can stand upright. Cylinders and cones are the perfect shapes to make a space-rocket pencil holder.

Wow!
Any slice across a sphere has a circular face, but not all the faces are the same size.

Make and decorate a pencil holder

YOU WILL NEED
empty kitchen roll, ruler, scissors, coloured card, glue, tape, felt pen

1 First cut the empty kitchen roll to size – it should be about 12 cm long. Cut a piece of card large enough to cover it. Glue this over the kitchen roll, then decorate it to look like a rocket.

the middle of the rocket is a cylinder

2 Cut out two circles of card about 15 cm across. Cut from the edge of each circle to the centre. Overlap each circle to make the cone-shaped top and base of your rocket. Stick in place with tape and decorate with felt pen.

the rocket top is cone shaped

24

3 To make the wings cut out another circle of card about 10 cm across. Fold it in half. Cut slits in the rocket as shown in the picture. Push the wings into the slits.

cut one slit here

cut one slit here

4 Stand your rocket on its base. Use tape to hold it in position. Place pens inside it and put on the rocket top!

BRAIN teaser

Challenge a friend to guess what shapes you will make when you slice up a cylinder.

First make a sausage shape from playdough. Cut off the ends to make a cylinder.

cut here

Make the cut shown above. What shape is the cut face? The answer is a circle.

cut here

What shape is the cut face this time? The answer is an ellipse.

cut here

Now what shape is the cut face? The answer is an oblong.

Finding grid references

It can be tricky finding your way around a town. Maps help because they show a big area as a small picture. On this map there is a grid of criss-crossing lines. Each square between the lines has a letter and a number. This gives a square its own name, such as A1 or C4.

Finding a grid reference

First find the ice-cream shop on the map. (It's at the bottom, by the red car.) Next, find the letter at the base of the column, beneath the ice-cream shop. It is B. Now find the number of the row alongside the ice-cream shop. It is 1. So the ice-cream shop is at B1.

1 Check out these grid references.

D6

C6

2 Now find the grid references for these places on the map.

bus stop

coffee shop

school

flower shop

Now try this

BRAIN teaser

Challenge a friend to copy and double the size of a picture using a grid. Here's how to do it.

First draw a grid on tracing paper. Tape it over the picture you want to copy.

Draw a second grid on ordinary paper. This should be twice the size of the first grid.

Now for the clever bit – carefully copy the picture onto the larger grid, square by square.

F   G   H   I   J

PROVE IT!

When you have a grid reference – as well as a grid – you can find what you are looking for.

This is a grid of a picnic table. Look at grid reference B4. You'll find a drink there. But watch out for grid references beginning with D. Can you see why?

27

Compass points

North, south, east and west are the points on a compass that help you find your way. On a compass, a magnetic needle always points north, so you can work out the other directions. Play this treasure hunt game. Look at the compass to check you're moving in the right direction.

Hunt the treasure game

YOU WILL NEED
ruler, scissors, card, pencil, coloured counters, small coin

1 For this game you will have to make a spinner, so cut out a 7 cm square of card. Decorate it as shown here. Push a pencil through the centre of your spinner.

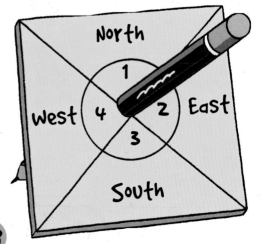

HOW TO PLAY

◆ This is a game for two to four players.

◆ First put the treasure, which is the coin, on one of the four islands. This is now the treasure island.

◆ Now, each player choose a different coloured counter. Put the counters on Central Harbour.

◆ Take turns spinning the spinner. Spin it once to find the direction to move in, then again to see how many squares to cross.

◆ When you can't follow the spinner's directions exactly, you can't move your counter until your next turn.

◆ The first to land on treasure island is the winner!

Get back on course go one square south then two squares east

Mermaid sings directions to you go one square east then one square south

Lost in a storm go back to Central Harbour

Message in a bottle go three squares east

Get back on course go three squares east

Dolphin shows you the way go one square south

Carried by a tidal wave to Pineapple Island

Mermaid sings directions to you go one square east then one square north

Get back on course go one square north then two squares east

Carried by a tidal wave to Mango Island

Get back on course go three squares south

Lost in a storm go back to Central Harbour

Get back on course go one square south then two squares west

Dolphin shows you the way go one square south

Message in a bottle go three squares south

Mermaid sings directions to you go one square west then one square south

COCONUT ISLAND

Hit jagged rocks miss a turn

PINEAPPLE ISLAND

Carried by a tidal wave to Banana Island

Bitten by a shark miss a go

Dolphin shows you the way go one square north

Lost in a storm go back to Central Harbour

START HERE

CENTRAL HARBOUR

Carried by a tidal wave to Pineapple Island

Carried by a tidal wave to Banana Island

Get back on course go three squares west

Message in a bottle go three squares north

Bitten by a shark miss a go

Message in a bottle go three squares west

BANANA ISLAND

Hit jagged rocks miss a turn

MANGO ISLAND

Lost in a storm go back to Central Harbour

Message in a bottle go three squares east

Dolphin shows you the way go one square north

Mermaid sings directions to you go one square west then one square north

Lost in a storm go back to Central Harbour

Get back on course go three squares north

Carried by a tidal wave to Coconut Island

Get back on course go one square north then two squares west

29

Useful words

angle
An angle is part of a complete turn. It is made where two straight lines meet.

angle

clockwise
This is when something moves around in the same direction as the hands on a clock.

face
The flat surface of a 3-D shape is called a face.
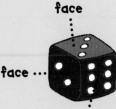
face
face ···
face

anti-clockwise
This is when something moves around in the opposite direction to the hands on a clock.

compass points
The main compass points are north, south, east and west. They help travellers find their way.

line symmetry
A shape with exactly matching halves has a line of symmetry.

line of symmetry

Name that shape

circle
This shape has one curved edge. Every place on its outline is the same distance from the centre.

oblong
This is a 2-D shape with two matching long sides, two matching short sides and four matching corners.

octagon
This is a 2-D shape with eight straight sides.

triangle
This shape has three straight sides that are all the same length. Other triangles have two sides the same length or all sides that are different lengths.

star
This straight-sided 2-D shape is called a star.

ellipse
This oval shape looks like a flattened circle.

pentagon
This is a 2-D shape with five straight sides.

cone
This 3-D shape has a flat face that is a circle and a curved surface that ends in a point.

square
This 2-D shape has four equal sides and four equal corners.

hexagon
A hexagon is a 2-D shape with six straight sides.

cylinder
This 3-D shape has two faces that are circles and one curved surface.

right angle

A right angle is a quarter of a complete turn. The corner of a square forms a right angle.

right angle

spiral

A spiral is a turn that winds further and further away from its starting point.

three dimensions (3-D)

Solid and hollow shapes are 3-D. They have three dimensions – length, width and depth.

length
width
depth

two dimensions (2-D)

Flat shapes are 2-D. They have only two dimensions – length and width.

length
width

---

cube

This is a 3-D shape with six square faces.

cuboid

This shape has six faces. They can all be oblongs. Or a cuboid can have two square faces and four oblong faces.

pyramid

This shape has triangular faces that meet at a point. Its base can be any straight-sided shape.

prism

triangular prism

hexagonal prism

The faces at the ends of a prism are exactly the same shape, size and distance apart along all sides. The end faces are joined together by oblongs.

sphere

This 3-D shape has one curved face and looks like a perfectly round ball.

Index

Notes for parents and teachers

This book is intended to help children become confident at recognising and making shapes and patterns. It also helps children to understand directions. Whenever we pack a lunchbox, choose a screwdriver or walk around the shops, we use our knowledge about shape, pattern, place and direction.

Shape

Our world is three dimensional: even sheets of paper and paint on a wall, have thickness or depth. Young children learn about shapes from the world around them. Help them build on this knowledge in the following ways:

- Look at and name shapes in your neighbourhood. What shape is a front door or a traffic cone?

- Discuss how shapes are appropriate for their use. A roof is often in the shape of a prism so that water flows off it easily. A broom handle is cylindrical. Its smooth surface makes it comfortable to hold. A triangle is a strong shape that's useful for holding up a heavy object such as a bridge.

- Encourage children to describe irregular shapes such as shells or rocks.

Pattern

A pattern is made by repeating shapes. When children make patterns, they learn about balance and symmetry. They also learn to predict how things will look. All these skills are useful for an understanding of art, design and technology.

- Help your child to find examples of symmetry in nature. Point out the broad symmetry and pattern in flowers, leaves, insects and snowflakes.

- Look closely for patterns in real life. Is there a pattern on your curtains or kitchen floor? See how many shapes they are made from and how the shapes fit together.

- Help children make up their own patterns when they decorate cards or make wrapping paper.

Place and direction

Understanding the direction of a turn, either clockwise or anti-clockwise, is the first step towards locating a place. The next steps are following compass directions and simple map reading. Here are ways to guide children:

- Look at local maps with children. Ask them to find their homes and schools.

- What's the shortest way to the park or zoo?

Praise and encourage

The most important thing is to not make maths seem like a chore. Show children maths is part of the everyday world, an important life skill, and that it can be great fun. Encourage children to work hard and praise the work they do. Then you'll help them have a positive approach to learning.